BORROWASH

BREAKFAST BOYS

BORROWASH

BREAKFAST BOYS

edited by Peter Dawson

The line drawing on the cover is by the late David Horobin.

Published by Peter Dawson
30 Elm Street
Borrowash
Derby, DE72 3HP

British Library Cataloguing-in-Publication data
A catalogue record for this book is available from the British Library

ISBN 978-1-5272-4760-4

Printed and bound by Jellyfish Solutions Ltd

THE BOYS

Andrew Alexander
Charles Bristow
Neil Clarke
Peter Dawson
Colin Dorman
Ian Frearson
Ray Hickling
Geoff Hooley
Bill Millichap
Andy Moore
Robert Plant
Ray Selby
Michael Shaw

I don't always understand what I am talking about but I know I'm right

Muhammad Ali

CONTENTS

FOOD FOR THOUGHT

Peter Dawson

The Duke of Wellington, victor at the Battle of Waterloo, always had regard to the logistics of food supply when it came to looking after his troops. He once asserted – and he was a very assertive sort of chap – that it was inviting disaster to send men into battle ill-fed and wondering where their next meal might be coming from.

George Bernard Shaw, in his play *Arms and the Man,* has a trooper say: 'You can always tell an old soldier by the inside of his holsters and cartridge boxes. The young ones carry pistols and cartridges: the old ones, grub'.

Shared meals have always played an important role in the history of human kind and are often a device which goes well beyond the simple matter of eating. When important foreign dignitaries visit the UK a banquet is laid on by the Queen to receive them. The food provided on such occasions, and the grandeur with which it is served, together constitute a device to honour those invited for blatantly political purposes. In courtship, the acceptability of one of those involved to the family of the other may be tested by an invitation to dinner, brilliantly depicted in the famous Spencer Tracy film *Guess Who's Coming to Dinner.*

One of the most critical points in the story of Jesus and his twelve disciples was the supper they shared as the climax of God's redemption plan for the world approached. Today, the Last Supper is remembered and celebrated in what we call the Eucharist or Holy Communion. When the disciples went fishing because they couldn't make sense of what was going on after Jesus' execution, there he was, in resurrected form on the shore of the Sea of Galilee. He had lit a fire and said to Simon Peter and the others, 'Bring some of the fish. Come and have breakfast'. Were they the very first breakfast boys?

With the development of what may be called the separated family, with members eating at different times, sometimes in different locations in the home, and maybe even having different food, opportunities for bonding decline.

Some years ago, one of the teachers' unions stated that children at school learned more readily and behaved better if they were provided with a good breakfast in a quiet environment. A harassed mother protested that she had no time for that. 'It's chaos in our house in the morning with four kids. It's everyone for themselves and they just have to grab what they want and run'.

The grab-it-and-run approach does not apply in the case of the breakfast boys of Borrowash, a village a few miles outside Derby. All are connected in one way or another with the local Methodist Church. They meet once a month at a local coffee house and bakery called Caffe Torte. There they tell one another about life's happenings and exchange opinions on putting the world to rights. Sometimes individuals adopt the sort of approach used by Muhammad Ali in expressing their opinions.

In the pages of this book there are stories some of the boys have written, both real and fictional; memories some have shared; jokes some have told; bits and pieces of this and that picked up over the years. So, dear reader, you will find here truths about life, accounts of triumphs and disasters, and plenty to make you laugh. You may also, perhaps, find something of your own story in what the breakfast boys have shared.

I have resisted a schoolmasterly temptation to interfere with writers' different styles, for example in punctuation and the use of capital letters.

My special thanks to Ian Frearson for driving this project forward. Also to my wife, whose professional secretarial skills continue to amaze me after witnessing it for many years. Watching her type up an MS without once looking at the keyboard is to witness a rare and disappearing skill.

Peter Dawson

THE STORIES

GIRL POWER

Ian Frearson

When the first of the leaflets appeared at my place on the breakfast table I automatically assumed there was a simple mistake and slid it across towards the girl's side. 'She who Must be Obeyed' looked amused and slid it back with a short 'it's for you'. I looked again. The first and most imposing words of the front page indicated Ockbrook W.I. Annual Competition. I was intrigued to determine on what grounds I had been singled out, as most deserving, to receive such a document. In a fit of pique at not being told spontaneously I threw it into the recycling.

The next day there it was again. It was the sort of conundrum that had to be bottomed and bottom it was something I had now determined to do. It shortly transpired, following some little questioning and a lot of laughter at my expense, that both Anne and Madeleine, wife and daughter, had considered that I had bragged enough about my jam making to put money where mouth was and so had entered me for the local W.I. Jam making competition.

On this occasion damsons were out of season but I was determined that, if I was to enter at all, it should include a pot of of damson plus, a special recipe of my own containing an all important but secretive ingredient. Having committed myself I did not want to prejudice the judges by appearing as a man, so made up a suitable female nom-de-pot in order to put me on an equal footing. I designed and printed labels, selected two equal, if not identical, jars. Carefully applied circular tops, painstakingly cut with pinking shears from two different, but tastefully suitable, bolts of material, filled in the form and awaited the day. This dawned bright and clear, with every prospect of good fortune.

Collectively we took our offerings to the place with high hopes of success and no moral thoughts of faked identity. To gain entry to the building was like attempting to break into Fort Knox. Four doors had to be negotiated, each with a guard of frighteningly stern visage and ample proportions. The last one, actual entry to the exhibition hall, was barred by a large lady in something akin to a bell tent, who loudly informed us that no one, and she meant no one, was going to get past her until all exhibits had been placed. To allow this to happen she had three runners, whose job it was to take the offerings and place them in their appropriate position. On completion of this explanation she summoned one of her runners with a loud 'Cissy!'

A diminutive figure, thin as a stick and bent almost double, crept slowing down the side tables towards the receptor. This it transpired was 'the runner' upon whom the task fell to take our offerings and who, with some difficulty in maintaining both balance and hold on the precious entries, set off arachnid like across the hall.

Later that day we revisited in order for me to claim my prizes. No such luck. I had been judged and found wanting. There were the three winning rosettes on three jars of jam but with mine, only cards on which a spidery hand gave comment and advice on my efforts. I was at a loss to judge whether or not my nom-de-pot subterfuge had been rumbled. I was assured by the females of the family that this was not the case and that I should accept the judgement with good grace and just try harder next time. I still wonder if there is more to the comments than meets the eye. On both cards it read something on reflection of which I later could not help but think we could all do. All it said was 'Presented well on the outside but needs more attention on the inside'. Just like me on a good day, I thought.

TESTING MR BERTRAM

Andy Moore

They say schooldays are the happiest days of your life. There was certainly fun to be had. One of our particular favourite pastimes involved Mr Bertram our woodworking and technical drawing teacher.

Mr Bertram was a very tall beanpole of a man usually attired in his brown woodworking coat and upon leaving his office completed by a flat cap. The main thing about Mr B. though was how funny it was to see him lose his temper. This of course became our goal whenever we had technical drawing.

On some occasions we succeeded fantastically resulting in tables and chairs being sent flying or the big wooden set squares for use on the blackboard being flung at some errant pupil, all of which caused nothing but belly aching laughter amongst the class. At other times he could remain, annoyingly for us, completely, or seemingly so to us, completely at calm with whatever we tested him with.

On one such occasion he was late arriving to the lesson so, with nothing better to do, we decided to stick as many drawing pins or anything sharp we could find through the underside of his seat so that they protruded onto where he would place his posterior. As soon as he entered the classroom we watched with anticipation only to experience no reaction, not one word – a disappointment to us all.

He had quite a collection of plants around the classroom and we took it upon ourselves to fill the large sink, in the corner of class, with water and drown the plants, but yet again, on discovering his sunken garden, he calmly pulled the plug, carried on teaching and then slowly replaced the plants in their former positions around the classroom without uttering a word on the matter.

One final example of his refusal to take the bait dangled in front of him occurred one snowy winter's day. Again he left the room for some reason and left to our own devices we hatched a plan. As it was a ground floor classroom two of our class slid open the window, climbed out and started piling up the snow. The snow was passed inside in scooped handfuls until every desk drawer was as full as possible, we then closed the drawers, the two friends clambered back through the window and all returned to our seats we waited. On returning to the room Mr B. sat down and resumed teaching, whether he noticed something awry or maybe the snow was melting, he suddenly opened a drawer pulled it out of the desk, calmly walked to the sink emptied the drawer of snow, walked back to the desk and repeated another two times. Nothing, no reaction, no outburst, no hurling of objects but, in all us students a quiet satisfaction in his solitary walk to the sink and back.

And yet at other times the slightest wrong movement could provoke our longed for reaction. In my two years of taking technical drawing we were like small creatures trying to draw our prey out of hiding. We didn't always get there but, as I say, it was fun trying and when we did, oh the joy.

MUSIC FOR BREAKFAST OR ANY TIME

Andy Moore

Pieces of music that touch my heart in one way or another:

Josef Suk (1874–1935) Asrael Symphony, composed after the death of his father-in-law Dvorak and his wife, Dvorak's daughter.

Pyotr Tchaikovsky (1840–1983) Symphony No. 6, hauntingly beautiful, first performed nine days before his death.

Sergei Rachmaninov (1873–1943) Symphony No. 2, A beautiful soaring work, full of passion and wonderful absorbing melodies.

Frederick Delius (1862–1943) violin Concerto, a lovely piece of music, lyrical, pastoral just poetic.

Nikolai Rimsky-Korsakov (1844–1908) Antar, a symphonic suite which I just find wonderful to listen to.

Ralph Vaughan Williams (1872–1958) The Lark Ascending, the most beautiful evocative piece of music, sublime in every way.

Nikolai Myaskovsky (1881–1950) Symphony No. 6, considered his magnum opus; an intense and to me moving piece.

Bedrich Smetana (1824–1884) Ma Vlast, a beautiful suite of music depicting his Czech homeland.

FOUR IN A BED

Ray Hickling

My wife and I got married a few months after I finished university, so we could only afford a couple of nights in London as a honeymoon. However, with some serious saving, the following summer we were able to do a coach tour to the Austrian Tyrol and stayed in a lovely village called Tarenz, not too far from Innsbruck. As was common in the 60's, some folk were farmed out to sleep in local houses, but we were fortunate enough to have a room in a new extension to the hotel. There was, alas, no evening entertainment in Gasthof Lamm, but we discovered that a hotel further up the mountain had a cellar bar with a band – whoopee!

We were told by the holiday rep that although the front door to the hotel would be locked around 10pm, there was a door at the back which was left open for late revellers. On that basis, we decided to join some others who were sleeping out on foray to experience the delights of the band – which was so delightful, it got rather late and we ended up picking our way down the mountain in darkness, passing the very eerie church yard where many of the graves had flickering candles on them!

Having bid goodnight to our companions as they went to the houses where they were sleeping, we arrived back at the hotel, but, as you've probably guessed, could not find the open door. We tried throwing pebbles at the rep's bedroom window, to no avail, so were thinking 'what on earth do we do now'. Well, in the course of conversation earlier with a young couple from Mansfield, similar in age to us, they had been telling us about the enormous bed they had, big enough for four, they said!! So, off we set back up the hill, in the hopes of rousing them and sharing this bed and, I'm glad to say, as even the summer nights were chilly, this we managed to do – share a bed with two people we had only met a few days before! There was, however, one small problem – the lady of the house spoke very little English, so we had to sneak out at daybreak, before she was up and around, so as to avoid a very awkward confrontation.

However, the most hilarious bit was yet to come, as this English couple – all dressed up in their finery, as you did to go out in those far off days – are walking down the hill at around 5.45am being greeted by all the locals going up the hill to early morning Mass at the church. Needless to say, there was an open door – but not where we thought it was in the dark. Fifty years on we still fondly remember our four in a bed experience!!

THE CARAVAN

Charles Bristow

(as narrated to another breakfast boy)

For a number of years my brother and sister-in-law owned a caravan that was kept by the sea in Essex. He was by profession a geologist, she a geography teacher. His job was producing geological maps of various areas of England and for a period it was the turn of Essex. Since their family home was in Beckenham it was temporarily more commodious for them to live on the job, hence the caravan. This was occupied during the week but at week-ends they regularly decanted back to the high life of Beckenham.

It had not gone unnoticed. The residents of an adjacent caravan, a much older couple than they, politely enquired if the van might be available at week-ends for their twin sons to visit. It was agreed that, providing they did not require it, and it was left in a tidy manner, they had no objection to their sons using it to visit their parents.

The Monday following the first occasion, brother and sister-in-law returned to their mobile work retreat and were delighted to discover a new crisp five-pound note on the table. These were the days when a fiver was a weekly wage for some and could secure: a week's petrol for the car, comestibles for two, an evening of entertainment and still have some left for non essentials such as rent. The caravan was found to be immaculate and the tone set for the season, the Monday fiver continuing to appear each week. All continued to go swimmingly well for a considerable time and both parties seemed to be very well satisfied with the arrangements.

One Monday morning they returned to the site to find things as expected but were then blessed by a surprise visit from the twin sons' mother. She explained to them that the police had been round during the weekend and asked if they knew where the occupants of the caravan were since they wanted access to look found. She carefully went on to explain that, despite having a key, she would not let on and so had not granted them the access they wanted. Brother and sister-in-law thanked her profusely but wondered why the constabulary should take such an interest in their particular caravan.

Weeks passed. The arrangement continued and each Monday morning the fiver appeared on the caravan's little folding table. It was only some months later, after the mapping project was completed and the caravan had been moved on, that the truth emerged and the interest of the long arm of the law in their property became almost a family joke. It became apparent that the couple from the adjoining caravan, whose twins had used their own accommodation so regularly during many week-ends and for which they had been compensated so lavishly, were a certain Mr and Mrs Kray.

BLOOD ON MY DESERT KHAKI

Peter Dawson

In the USA, they say that everyone knows where they were when President Kennedy was assassinated. He had just been hugely encouraged by his reception in Dallas, but disaster struck just when things were going well.

Heading into the centre of Dallas, the presidential motorcade slowed to take a sharp turn below the Texas School Book Depository at Dealey Plaza. Harvey Oswald, high up in the building, took careful aim through the telescopic sight on his rifle and blew the President's brains out. A good day turned into one of horror and disaster.

Such was my experience one day after leaving school at eighteen to join the RAF. Autumn 1951. Trees on the high ground overlooking RAF Credenhill, near Hereford, were dressed in a breathtaking range of browns and golds. Oh, to be in England now that autumn's here. But my destiny was to leave these gloriously colourful scenes for the Egyptian desert.

Just out of the grammar school sixth form, where keeping a balance between rugby, cricket and the debating society on the one hand and GCE Advanced Levels on the other tested my priorities, the brave new world of National Service in the RAF looked inviting. It was to present me one day with the most devastating experience of my life; one that has left a permanent imprint on my beliefs.

Recruit training at Credenhill, known colloquially as square bashing, was an astonishing experience. Freddie Truman, a frighteningly fast bowler from Yorkshire who had been denied postponement of his National Service despite having been selected to play for England in the West Indies, sat on the end of his bed the first night and, at great length, swore at the MoD. It made me realize my unpreparedness for life in the real world – many of the swear words were unknown to me. Someone laid a bet, challenging his fellow recruits to tip Freddie out of bed during the night. One chap was prepared to take up the challenge. The rest of us thought he was a fool but, if he was of a mind to avoid National Service by getting bashed up by Fiery Fred and crippled for life, his foolhardiness might do the trick.

After lights out, we peered from behind our blankets to see what would happen. The chap who had taken up the challenge tipped Freddie out of bed and shot out the door, hotly pursued by England's future cricketing star. We waited for the return of the foolhardy fellow who had turned Freddie's bed over. We expected much blood. But chaser and chased returned the best of pals. 'What happened?', we asked. Truman replied, in his tough Yorkshire patois: 'I caught booger, put 'im down and asked 'im what were bloody bet. He said ten quid. We thought a fiver each would be about right, so I didn't bash 'im'. I thought to myself that life in the RAF was going to be an exciting education.

Another dramatic development was imminent. Hoping to avoid spending two years in some uninteresting job in the UK, I was delighted to be selected for flying control. My training was to take place in the control tower at RAF Mauripur near Karachi in Pakistan. I was going to see the world and spend my time with aeroplanes. Hooray!

Flown out from Lyneham with a number of other newcomers to the RAF, we arrived at a tented transit camp at El Hamra, near the Suez Canal. This was at the beginning of the 1950s, just a few years from the time when Sir Anthony Eden decided upon an invasion of Suez by British troops. The atmosphere at El Hamra was tense, with local Arabs taking pot shots at anyone venturing out into the nearby desert. RAF personnel stationed at El Hamra carried arms at all times, even when off duty in the station cinema. Sitting among men with rifles between their knees was something new. It made going to the pictures to see a Doris Day musical a strange experience.

The six of us who were sharing a tent were a motley crew. Harry had the biggest personality. A tall, suave chap with a posh voice, educated at a public school, he had views on everything and loudly expressed them at every opportunity. It was no surprise to learn that he intended to go on the stage. He claimed to have a place at RADA awaiting the completion of his military service.

After breakfast one morning, the six of us were called up over the tannoy to report to the armoury. Equipped with rifles and clips of ammunition, we were to provide the rear guard of a convoy going down the road beside the canal to Ismailia. But as we were climbing aboard the open lorry from which we were to keep a look-out for hostiles, I was told to return my arms and pack my kit ready for departure to Pakistan. While on the whole glad to be moving on, I was a shade disappointed to be denied the chance of desert heroics. The achievements of the desert rats in the war against Hitler had always excited me. I rather liked the idea of being like those who chased Rommel across North Africa. My immaturity was about to be brought home to me.

In what seemed no time at all, and before I had left the scene, the vehicle in which my breakfast companions had driven off was back. It struggled slowly, grindingly, through the station gate in an advanced state of destruction. There were bullet holes the length of the vehicle, with blood flowing from some of then. Harry and the other four men with whom I had shared a tent and breakfasted were all dead. Harry, with his thespian ambitions, had rather fancied himself as good-looking. He wasn't now. His head had been blown off by a rocket from a bazooka and only the stump of his neck remained. Without thinking what I was doing, I stepped forward to help unload the bodies and ended up with blood and guts on my recently acquired unblemished desert khaki.

I was not long out of the security of a grammar school in a leafy part of Kent, the garden of England, with little experience of real life. For the first time, I realized that armed conflict was not just an adventure used by film makers to sell their products; it was a heartbreaking business. Like those whose dead bodies I helped unload, I was just eighteen years old and deeply affected. Memorable? Yes, devastatingly so. For many years, I was unable to speak of the never-to-be-forgotten horror witnessed one morning in the sands of Egypt when a good day turned into one of horror and disaster.

Now, more than eighty years of age, that period in my oh-so-young life erupts in my mind when reports of desert conflict appear in the news, not least when one hears of young soldiers being blown up in the sands of Afghanistan. News reports say that some traumatized troops need counselling when they return home. I know just how they feel.

BLACKPOOL CAPERS

Ray Hickling

More years ago than I care to remember, before we were married, we embarked on a trip to Blackpool, with our good friends Ron and Rosemary, to see the famous illuminations. Having got there, parked, and had a bit of a wander, we decided to have some fish and chips – as you would in Blackpool! As we had finished ours, my other half had the bright idea of going down onto the beach, despite the fact that it was largely bathed in darkness, being in the shadow of the promenade. So, while our friends were finishing their chips, we tripped merrily down the steps to the beach, along with a small boy with similar intentions.

What we did not know, nor could see, at the bottom of the steps there was a HUGE puddle of water into which we stepped – waist deep – and small child disappears! Ron and Rosemary are somewhat alarmed by our shrieks and small boy's sister is shouting, 'Jeremy, where are you?' Only when we managed to scramble out of the puddle, having first rescued poor Jeremy, did we realise that there was a plank across the water; but at least we managed to stop our friends suffering the same fate.

Having made it back up on to the prom, as we were walking back to the car park, the searchlight on the top of the Tower seemed to be continually playing on us and illuminating our soggy, dripping lower halves for all the world to see. When we get back to the car, we have to strip off and huddle under a car blanket, while Rosemary had my trousers trapped in the car window, blowing in the wind, to try and dry them off a bit – until, that is, we saw a police car, and she thought they might be less than sympathetic!

I have to say, that was our one and only – but unforgettable – trip to Blackpool!

HOLOCAUST HAIKU

Peter Dawson

Haiku has its origins in Japanese writings. Its classical form has three unpunctuated verses of three lines in the strophic form 5.7.5. A word in each verse has a natural link with a word in the next. In the following haiku the linking words are times of the year – spring, summer and winter. My father Judah Dawson, who was part Jewish, had distant relatives who died in the Holocaust. He chose to be called by his second name, Richard, because, as he put it: 'We're not going to no concentrated camp'.

Spring in the death camp
Was a dark time for us Jews
Gas ovens roaring

Summer was as bad
Heavy was the curse on us
Each day that season

So that was Auschwitz
In our hearts always winter
Hate still haunts Hebrews

ANTITHESIS

Robert Plant

Rob Plant is greatly impressed by a sermon by Martin Luther King entitled A Tough Mind and a Tender Heart. It is based on the words of Jesus in Matthew 10 v 16: 'Be ye therefore wise as serpents and harmless as doves'.

'The tough mind is sharp and penetrating, breaking through the crust of legends and myth . . . sifting the true from the false. The tough-minded individual is astute and discerning. He has a . . . firmness of purpose and solidness of commitment. Who doubts that this toughness of mind is one of man's greatest needs? . . . There is an almost universal quest for easy answers and half-baked solutions. Nothing pains some people more than having to think.

'But we must not stop with the cultivation of a tough mind. The gospel also demands a tender heart. Tough mindedness without tender-heartedness is cold and detached, leaving one's life in a perpetual winter devoid of the warmth of spring and the gentle heat of summer. What is more tragic than to see a person who has risen to the disciplined heights of tough mindedness but at the same time has sunk to the passionless depths of hardheartedness?

'Jesus reminds us that the good life combines the toughness of the serpent and the tenderness of the dove. To have serpentlike qualities devoid of dovelike qualities is to be passionless, mean, and selfish. To have dovelike without serpentlike qualities is to be sentimental, anemic, and aimless. We must combine strongly marked antitheses'.

HOT DATE

Ian Frearson

Some years ago, in the pretty Cornish town of Liskeard, an almost indecent event ran through and very nearly cracked the central society of churchgoers. It had started as a rumour that had quickly spread until the whole settlement was talking about it and many talking about acting on it. The whole thing had begun one warm summer's day when thoughts should have been concentrated on dips in the sea and long cool glasses of ginger beer. Instead people were aggressively occupied with a notice that had appeared in the local free paper that was scandalous.

Identification of the perpetrator was the next course of action. People who had, up to now, scarcely found time to exchange a civil greeting with each other now stood and exchanged opinions on the topic, in loud aggressive tones, right there in the streets. Nothing was going to stop them from finding out the source of the notice and of course punishing the offender.

Never was a topic more loudly or vociferously

discussed and never before in living history of the community were opinions so dramatically affected. Eyes welled with tears of emotion as spinster and bride alike discussed how they would deal with someone who could even consider sullying their beloved and devoted settlement with this sort of common diatribe. The only problem was, the thought of doing something was tempered by the need to find someone who would have the temerity to do it: this was the root of the dilemma.

But what, I can hear your brain asking itself without response, was the cause of the problem. Well, shortly and simply, it was this. A notice under Personal in the Liskeard Gazzette had been headed SBFS – translated, standing for Single Black Female Seeks. Now this alone led to rapid drawings of breath among certain groups. To advertise for a mate so openly smacked of tarty or smutty. But the reader who was brave enough to read on found the following:

> *SINGLE BLACK FEMALE seeks male companionsip, ethnicity unimportant. I'm a very good girl who LOVES to play. I love long walks in the woods, riding in your pickup truck, hunting, shooting, camping and fishing trips, cosy winter nights lying by the fireside with you. Candlelight dinners will have me eating out of your hand. I'll be at the front*

door when you get home from work. Call 01272-642370 and ask for Annie, I'll be waiting.

The staff of the offending newspaper were tight-lipped over the advertisement. It seemed there was only one thing to do, but no one it appeared had the guts or the gall to do it. After a few days of intense bickering, one man decided to take the bull by the horns and confront the demon, whatever it would be that awaited him. It was of course the Methodist Minister who decided that if no one else could do it then he would, even and only for the sake of a closure on the matter. With some trepidation and with trembling hands he dialled the number, not knowing and hardly wanting to know what would await him. His hands trembled as the number rang out for a while, then he heard a soft gentle female voice answer with the words 'Hallo moi deer, Truro RSPCA'.

PARAKEETS ON THE WINDOWSILL

Neil Clarke

Jean was offered the use of a bungalow her boss owned at Terrigal near Sydney as a base for a holiday in Australia during September. Wow! What an offering! We happily accepted, wondering about the logistics and how to get there. The adventure of a lifetime followed.

When we in due course reached Terrigal it was bigger than we expected. We were pretty tired with all the travelling but there was food waiting for us on arrival. An even better welcome from some Parakeets on the kitchen windowsill. They are like parrots and were bright green and red. Having settled in we went down to the seafront to have a look at the beach. Children had just come out of school and were already on the boogie board. Then we ventured into the shopping mall to buy something for tea. We then phoned our daughter and were in bed by 7.30pm, exhausted!

The following morning, we rang our son, who didn't want to talk to us – just kept saying 'Put the

TV on'. We couldn't understand why. How could the same programme be on an Australian TV and a British one? But we had landed in Australia on 11 September 2001 but were 12 hours ahead of UK time and 17 hours ahead of the time in New York but the tragic events of 9-11 had happened whilst we were sleeping. The main priority for Aussies was that their Prime Minister was in New York, so the country was being run by the Deputy PM. That was their main focus!

One day we went from Terrigal to Gosford and caught the train to Sydney Central station then on to Circular Quay, which is between the Harbour Bridge and the Opera House. We were able to go inside the Opera House and booked for Saturday night's performance of Stravinsky's 'Firebird'. It is a truly magnificent building with fantastic acoustics. Then we went on a replica of the 'Bounty' made for the film 'Mutiny on the Bounty' and were entertained with local history landmarks. The men on board were then press-ganged into hauling down the sails, followed by a lovely fish buffet, which turned out to be chicken, whilst we sailed around the harbour. We returned to Terrigal on a train that took one and a half hours, so for commuters it makes it a long journey to and from work.

The following day we returned to Sydney and looked out over the Harbour, watching people climbing the bridge. We already had tickets to make the climb. The experience was fantastic! We had a rigorous training session. Watching a film and being breath-tested and passing health checks before being allowed to proceed to the 'kitting-out stage! We weren't allowed anything in our pockets and had to remove our watches. We were then taken to a 3-sided rail and instructed how to attach ourselves to the rails on the side of the bridge. Then we were issued with radios, earpieces, hankies and fleeces. We then followed the instructor out of the training area, down the street to the bottom of the tower and entered a door to begin the climb up a lot of stairs. This was very relaxed and any bits that stuck out were covered in yellow foam and we each had to warn the following person about these.

Tim, our guide, led us up the bridge. Every so often we stopped to take in the view. When we got to the top Tim took photos of the group and individual groups at strategic points, with the Opera House and the Sydney Skyline in the background or the sea below us. The climb up and down the bridge took three hours and we enjoyed every step. It was a truly wonderful experience. Once back on terra firma we found a tiny cafe and ordered a fish basket which was mainly squid and other rubbery bits!

The next day we decided to stay in the local area, visiting the next bay known as Avoca which was good for surfers. We explored inland and found a Fragrant Garden with lots of twists and turns, seats and pagodas and archways, in quite a small area really. It was magical with poems and plaques everywhere. As it was springtime there were daffodils, bluebells and irises and of course Fairies running about. There was a birthday party in progress with a Fairy Godmother telling stories to the children. It was absolutely fantastic and we spent quite a leisurely time in the relaxed atmosphere. All girls and one batman who would not join in the fun!

Brenda, who managed the bungalow we stayed in, invited us to visit her at Empire Bay. She took us to various bays, including a ferry trip to Palm Beach where they filmed the outdoor scenes for 'Home and Away'. We had noticed a 'Uniting Church of Australia' which had advertised a service to mark a 'National Day of Prayer' in memory of all those affected by the 9-ll attacks in the USA. We decided to attend. We parked as close as we could to the church. We think there were about 1,000 people in there. It had moveable walls that retracted into a huge hexagon. Extra chairs were brought in and yet there were still people standing, even in the glass entrance. Yet people stood up, insisting that we sit, because we were visitors and we were welcomed as representatives of the whole world who were all sharing in their grief.

It was a very positive rather than a formal service. A mother stood up and told us about her daughter.

She had never passed any exams but had worked her way up in the finance industry until she became a trainer for those working in the cut-throat world of trading. She had been on the 105th floor of the World Trade Centre in New York when the plane had hit the Twin Towers. The mother was sure her daughter would not have survived the attack but thanked God for her happy life.

Then a Fire Fighter stood up and explained that for the Australian State of New South Wales there were 350 Fire Fighters and this was the number of firemen that had died trying to rescue people.

Then a little girl, aged 7, came to the front with her Dad. Her best friend was visiting New York and her family were worried because they had not heard from them. The Minister invited all the children to come to the front, around forty, and the girl explained all they had planned to see, including the Twin Towers. As you know, the area where the Towers' debris fell was vast. The whole time images of the Twin Towers and the planes hitting and the consequent billowing smoke were being projected high up on the front area – randomly. It was an incredibly powerful and moving service with no hymns, just prayers.

One day we travelled to Calga Spring Animal Sanctuary, which was owned by a former Australian Minister of the Environment. It covers 80 acres and we arrived just as three bus loads of noisy children drew up in the car park. We decided to go around just before the children but did not know what we were looking at, or the significance of what we were seeing. After lunch, the guide, Adam, offered to take us round on our own. Being a lot quieter, we saw much more than before: that included three types of wallabies and two sorts of finches. There were many aboriginal paintings in the caves surrounding the enclosures. These markings were explained, especially the significance of the hand print that had the wedding ring finger missing. Apparently, the husband bound it at the base and after time it dropped off!

The whole place was surrounded by two rings of fences, to keep out the non-indigenous Australian wildlife, rabbits and foxes. Unfortunately, as we made our way to the car, we were confronted by an emu that had got through the inner ring of the fencing. I went back into the office to let the guide know and was given a bucket of food, while he went off to find Adam. Our job was to feed and entertain Pauline the emu. Our eyes were on the same level as Pauline's. I don't know who was more intimated, Pauline or us. Adam eventually appeared with the guide and they thought it would be easy to get her back into the enclosure. It took at least ten minutes to get her inside the fence.

That was our last full day in Terrigal, so we had one last trip to the beach, then bought a fish supper to have back at the bungalow. Before returning to Sydney we had enough time to do some last minute shopping at Erina Fair, realising we were more likely to get local indigenous items. We then travelled back to Sydney via the district of Blakenhurst, which is very near Botany Bay, where Captain Cook and his crew landed over 200 years ago. The next day we celebrated our wedding anniversary driving in Australia to hand back the hire car at the airport and checked in for our flight to Cairns. What happened next is another story, So you will have to wait to find out all about it. G'day to all you Poms!

ALL SORTS OF STUFF

The boys were encouraged to submit, inter alia, a few sentences on the best and happiest moments in their careers, their favourite jokes and quotations, and anything else of interest.

Robert Plant says a neutron walks into a bar and says, 'How much for a drink?' The bartender replies, 'For you, there's no charge'.

Michael Shaw says the best moment in his career was telling the boss in 1968 what he could do with his offer of a halfpenny wage rise. Another dramatic moment in his life was sitting on the end of the bed on his wedding night, looking at £2 and ten shillings in his hand – the only money he possessed – and asking himself: 'What the hell have I done?'

Geoff Hooley tells of a friend with a five-year-old daughter who was taken to church by her grandparents. The person leading the service was about to start a prayer when Emma peeped and saw that her grandfather still had his eyes open. Her little voice cried out, 'Don't start. Grandad's not gone to sleep yet'.

Andy Moore goes in for rewriting well known proverbs and sayings:

Where there's a will there are cash hungry relatives.

Don't put off till tomorrow what you can put off for a lifetime.

Desperate times call for a trip to the loo.

Those who live in glasshouses should probably move.

Out of small acorns grow fat squirrels.

It's the early bird that gets the worm, but probably doesn't see the cat coming.

Bill Millichip handed in thirty jokes to the editor. Here are six that made me groan even more than the others:

I've made a film about the world's longest truck. You should see the trailer.

I rang up British Telecom and said: 'I want to report a nuisance caller'. He said: 'Not you again!'

I was reading this book today, The History of Glue. I couldn't put it down.

This policeman came up to me with a pencil and a piece of very thin paper. He said, 'I want you to trace someone for me'.

I told my mum that I'd opened a theatre. She said, 'Are you having me on?' I said, 'Well I'll give you an audition, but I'm not promising you anything'.

This cowboy walks in to a German car showroom and he says 'Audi!'

Finally, from Bill, there's one that is no joke:

War does not determine who is right; it determines who is left.

Here are some of Peter's favourite quotations:

All things are possible to those who believe.

Jesus Christ

Men are not made for safe havens.

Aeschylus 500BC

If you are waiting for the right time to start work, it's now

Eaton Square School 2015

Quae dant, quaeque negant, gaudent tamen esse rogatae

Whether they give or refuse, women are glad to have been asked

Publius Ovid 40BC

IDIOTIC OCCASIONS

Andy Moore

There are times in life when all our common sense seems to leave us and for want of a better phrase we appear to be complete idiots. I have in my life succumbed to this phenomenon on several occasions.

Once, in the 1970s, upon leaving a football match against our close rivals, a game which my team had won, there was a lot of fighting outside the ground. As I walked past with my dad and brother, engrossed in the scenes happening on my right, I was completely oblivious of the Victorian cast iron lamppost which, firmly standing its ground, knocked me to the floor, leaving me in a worse state than any of the violence happening in the distance. The occasion left me suspicious of lampposts ever since.

Slightly later in my childhood, my friends and I decided it would be a good idea to jump over the border of one of my friend's gardens and forward roll off the top of the wall the other side of the border and land on the pavement outside about two feet below. This went well a few times but as I took my next turn I overshot the wall and instead of putting my hands out for some reason just headbutted the pavement beneath me, a bone jarring sensation I can still feel now, and an event which some people say explains a lot.

Moving on to my teenage years I well remember how my attempts at impressing a girlfriend backfired. We were in the kitchen at home, my mum was also in attendance. I had been making a cake of some long forgotten flavour and the electric whisk was lying around on the worktop. Before I go any further I should just mention that I have always had quite long hair, which is quite pertinent to what happened next. In a moment of above mentioned idiocy I decided to mimic shooting myself in the temple with the whisk . . . and upon pressing the trigger, which in reality was the on switch, proceeded to whisk my hair into the biggest tangle imaginable and appearing to pull half my hair out of one side of my head, though I did manage to stop short of scalping myself. It was, if I may say, not one of my brightest moments.

When they were building a new house at the end of our street we used to use the building site as a playground which resulted in quite a few moments of bad decisions. A friend decided to jump from the upstairs floor to the bottom, as there was as yet no staircase, resulting in two broken wrists. As for me, well we had the stupid idea of a sand fight which resulted in me spending the whole summer as a pirate due to the scratched eyeball, meaning I had to wear an eye patch. On top of that we were running around in the skeleton of the house, when all of a sudden I felt a searing pain in my foot. On further investigation I found a block of wood attached to the heel of my shoe. On even further investigation, I found that the reason the block of wood was attached to my shoe was because a six inch nail attached to the wood had attached itself to my foot, so I valiantly clomped my way home where the block was painfully detached along with the nail. This resulted in a trip to the doctors for a tetanus shot.

These are just a few of my lapses into a less than desired state of existence. Well, I'm only human.

CANAL ADVENTURES

Geoff Hooley

Our first foray on the waterways of Britain was a Monday to Friday cruise from Middlewich to Chester. We'd decided that this route of about 25 miles and 18 locks would be suitable for us inexperienced sailors and shouldn't tax us too much. Also it was within easy reach of the boatyard if we got into any difficulty.

We hired a boat from Andersons at Middlewich and after being shown round the vessel and being instructed about various things we set off. Two of the staff came with us through the first three locks which are right next to the boatyard, giving valuable instruction on how to operate the locks.

After getting us to the first lock on the Middlewich branch, they departed and we were on our own. We did the next 10 miles and three more locks before mooring up for the night. The following day we safely negotiated our way up to Chester, mooring up before the short stretch down to the Northgate Staircase locks. We went for a walk to see what such locks were like. Usually the chambers are of equal size so that water will not be wasted when it passes from one chamber to the next. The locks themselves at Northgate are hewn out of the rock face and the chambers are not quite of equal size.

We were standing looking at the board at the side of the locks which explains how to go about operating them. If you're going down prepare by filling the top chamber and empty both the bottom chambers. If you're going up prepare by emptying the bottom chamber and filling the two top chambers.

As we were standing there reading the board a boat arrived into the top lock. Some crew members jumped off and tied up the boat and closed the lock gate that they had just passed through. For the locks to be set for their downward passage the two bottom locks had to be emptied, so the boat crew set about this. But the top chamber had rather a bad leak through the centre join of the gates and water was escaping at rather a fast rate into the second chamber.

The first we realised there was a problem was when a member of the clergy from Chester Cathedral who was walking his dog started asking if it was our boat in the lock. Our reply was of course, 'No', but we pointed him in the right direction as to whose it was. We went across to the chamber to find one steel narrowboat weighing about 15 tons in a lock where the water level had dropped being suspended on its ropes. They probably wouldn't take the weight much longer.

Before long members of the crew came running up to the boat and at first stood there wondering what to do. For some reason one of them foolishly thought that pulling on the ropes would stop it from falling. In the end the gates were opened to allow more water in to rectify the situation. We realised they were beginners like us. A nasty accident had been averted but it's easy to see how quickly these things can soon get out of hand. Had it not been for clergyman walking his dog there might have been a disaster.

On another of our adventures on the waterways we journeyed down the Shropshire Union canal or 'The Shroppie' as it is known. The canal runs from Ellesmere Port on the Mersey to Autherley Junction near Wolverhampton on the Staffs and Worcestershire canal. Not far out of Market Drayton is the Tyrley flight, a set of five locks surrounded by trees in a very pleasant setting. Regulating the water level in the pounds is done by a system of weirs. Some of the longer pounds discharge the excess water into a river or stream but at most locks there will be a weir which discharges into a side race which goes round the side of the lock. The side race at the bottom lock on the Tyrley flight runs very fast and discharges right on the entrance to the lock. The force of the water can push the boat sideways when passing the discharge.

To get the boat into the lock without being pushed sideways can be quite difficult, as we found out. Entering a lock at speed is not the easiest of manoeuvres, particularly when the width of the lock is just 7ft. The force pushed our boat sideways and we hit the wall with the bow, something which I'm sure many had done before us.

The rest of the flight went without a hitch and about 90 minutes later we emerged from the top lock ready for coffee. Someone was dispatched to put the kettle on and make the drinks. On entering the galley they were met by a sight that we could have done without. Over the floor of the galley was white powder and a blue canister lying beside it. What had happened? Well, the bang on the wall had knocked the fire extinguisher off its mounting and the handle hit the floor and discharged the contents. We did report the incident when we got back to the boatyard at the end of the holiday but they said not to worry as it wasn't the first time it had happened.

The Llangollen canal runs from Hurleston junction to the centre of Llangollen. It acts as an open aqueduct, taking in water from the river Dee at Horseshoe Falls to the Hurleston reservoir which supplies drinking water to a large part of Cheshire.

The canal thrived until the end of the First World War, after which it saw very little traffic and navigation was formally abandoned in 1944. The channel was retained as it still supplied water to the main line of the Shropshire Union, and the Cheshire Water Board. The Transport Act 1968 designated the canal as a cruiseway, and secured its future. The 11 mile (18km) stretch from Gledrid Bridge near Rhoswiel to Horseshoe Falls, including Pontcysylite and Chirk aqueducts, was designated a World Heritage site by UNESCO in 2009. The Pontcysylite aqueduct over the river Dee is the most outstanding feature along the canal. It carries the canal over the river in a cast iron trough 126ft above the river and is 1000ft long. It was built by Thomas Telford and was completed in 1805. It's the highest canal aqueduct in the world and is sometimes known as the 'waterway in the sky'. Boat trips are run from Llangollen over the aqueduct and back and are very popular. We had a couple of nights in Llangollen and decided to move to the bottom side of the aqueduct so that we could call in at the Chirk boatyard early the next morning.

The section from Llangollen to Trevor is in places quite bendy and narrow. We were getting towards Trevor and there were one or two fairly blind bends which require the sounding of the horn to let anybody coming in the opposite direction know that you are there. They in turn should sound their horn so that you are aware of them. We had duly sounded our horn and, not having heard any reply, assumed that the way ahead was clear so didn't reduce our speed. The bow of the boat was almost at the apex of the bend when the bow of the restaurant boat from Trevor came into view.

Boats are not like cars where when you hit the brake pedal the car stops almost in an instant. Your only means of stopping a boat is by going into reverse. Putting the boat in reverse is simple as most modern boats have a single lever control, so instead of the lever facing forwards you move it to face backwards. However there is a time delay between the propeller rotating forwards and changing to rotating backwards. During this delay the boat is still going forwards as you wait for the propeller to bite and actually start to move the boat backwards. By the time all this had happened, which was probably no more than about fifteen seconds, we had gone far enough forward to hit the restaurant boat midships.

On board the boat were a party of Japanese tourists having a meal. They thought it was hilarious that we had hit their boat. Out came their cameras to record the event and take home to their families to whom they would no doubt retell the event in great detail. We in the meantime had reversed back but the restaurant boat had just kept coming. I must admit I got a look that could kill from the woman on the back of the boat who was steering, but had she sounded her horn it wouldn't have happened.

THE JOURNEY

Ian Frearson

There is a school of thought that lives by the principle that it is better to travel hopefully than to arrive. Well, to travel hopefully would be a great opportunity, if not a miracle, on some journeys. There were many such that I endured during the late 1970s that are worthy of consideration and comment. One, the least clever and the most dangerous occurred whilst travelling up motorways – normally the notorious M6 – frequently on call outs to some rescue situation or other in the Lake District or across country towards North Wales. Anyway, a couple of cases in particular fit the bill and serve to show that it is a fine line between success and looking a prat.

The travel times to rescue call outs were always more than anticipated or hoped for since lives were almost always at stake and other traffic just served to slow us down seemingly deliberately. To relieve boredom, entertain younger family members and wind up other drivers we usually travelled in Land Rovers (stock Mountain Rescue vehicles) so the normal seating arrangement was three abreast in the front, similar behind.

When traffic frustrated us, and conditions allowed, we would change drivers on the move. The one sitting in the nearside seat would open the sliding window, climb out onto the roof, slide across then, as the one from the middle seat slipped across into the recently vacated nearside seat, the current driver would slowly and carefully slide towards the middle seat. This involved retaining one hand on the wheel and one foot on the accelerator until the very last moment, when the new driver slid feet first through the offside window and took over driving. By way of safety we always used piloting procedure and the incoming driver would say, 'I have control'. No harm done, good fun, boredom relieved and other motorists shocked and entertained.

The other case had started as a normal journey, albeit a potentially long and uncomfortable one, towards North Wales for a Mountain Rescue Team training week end. Even before we left Derby we knew it would not be a comfortable trip. Seven of us were crammed into an old long wheel based Land Rover, the day job for which was to carry plumbing tools and equipment. Steve sat in the middle with me at the window seat and Bill driving.

It was Bill's vehicle and ripe for mickey taking. It was spartan in every way with little by way of even essentials, let alone luxuries. Heating was not readily available but there were a series of buttons, rocker switches and pull stops, mostly useless, that Steve and I tested at random, all to the criticism and increasing rage of the driver. 'Leave it alone', was a favourite comment as we asked things like, 'What does this one do Bill?' Bill was getting increasingly frustrated with us and when Steve pumped one of the buttons and asked 'What's this one Bill?' he responded, 'Leave it alone, that is the windscreen wash'. Since nothing by way of water or wash had appeared on the screen, Steve said, 'But Bill, there's nothing happening'. Bill, rapier quick, responded, 'I know, it's dry clean'.

PLEASE LET IT BE YES

Charles Bristow

Pietra Fatunka was a good citizen of Poland who somehow got mixed up with the War (WWII that is) and finished up not knowing if they now lived in Poland or the hated Russia. He and his wife had lived through the awful times and had come through unscathed but for their terrible memories. They lived frugally but otherwise in comfort of each other's company in a small low browed cottage at the edge of woodland that contained mixed deciduous and coniferous trees from which they derived much of their daily living. Wild birds and animals added to their larder whilst fruits, herbs, and starchy roots gave them basic meals. This they supplemented by occasional trips to the nearest town – in reality a small parochial Russian village some 20 Kms away, from where they bought nothing but essentials.

One day, one fateful day, two men appeared outside their cottage, an appearance that gave them much concern. Some months before they had received a very official looking letter with a crown stamp and an embossed coat of arms that informed them the Government had decided to reconcile the boundary between Poland and Russia. They were terrified at the thought of being classified on the wrong wide of the boundary. For four days the men were sporadically in the distance, seemingly just walking around with poles and writing things in a large yellow book. 'How ironic' thought Pietri, 'It really should be a red book', but he kept his counsel to himself and prayed every night over the eventual outcome of the work.

On the fifth day Pietri and his short comfortable and plump wife were potting up pickles in store for the forthcoming season when there was an authoritative banging at the door. Pietri started, his wife squealed and raised a cloth to cover her face. Pietri, full of concern and impending doom, slowly approached the door and opened it to find a man in a long black leather coat just about to repeat the banging. The man had a thin sad looking face with a disagreeable expression that Pietri found unnerving and he immediately began to tremble uncontrollably. After a few seconds of being under scrutiny the man began to speak but Pietri, in his panic and fear, scarcely heard him until he heard the words '... and so the legal and official boundary has now been ratified and is to be just two metres on the far side of your garden. From now on you are officially in Poland'. There was a moment of consideration before recognition took hold and he burst into almost hysterical sobbing, with tears coursing down his cheeks as he slumped down the door frame and into a heap at the threshold.

The stranger looked on with some alarm until the old lady of the establishment appeared, when he enquired if the heap on the floor, sobs now slowly dying away, was alright. 'I think he will recover' said the old dame and began to lift her husband up from his semi-recumbant posture, and to his feet. When the sobbing had completely stopped the stranger turned to go, paused for a moment then turned back to face Pietri enquiring 'What made you so upset about the decision, are you sad about the outcome?' Pietri looked at him through tear filled eyes and quietly responded 'No, delighted' then before turning and closing the door added 'I could not stand another Russian Winter'.

ON THE WISDOM OF DADS

Robert Plant

After we got married, my father-in-law imparted a useful piece of wisdom: 'You know son, when you're trying for kids the best advice I can give you is that when my daughter becomes pregnant there'll likely be times when she'll be a complete @*l?# to you – just don't take it personally!' Understanding that changing hormones will impact the emotions of the one you love, with you at the sharp end, is a key part of being able to work through it.

My dad had already told me that once you have kids, finding the time to get things done, whether out in the yard or inside the house, would go out of the window. When I look back, I can appreciate why it took us so long to re-plaster and decorate, tile the floors and refit the kitchen; through expecting our first son to having our second. It's not just finding blocks of time to get jobs done, it's making allowances for how difficult it can be to work efficiently for want of a good night's sleep.

The governor of the Bank of England, in response to a question on what he thought when he woke in the morning, replied that he didn't wake in the morning anymore, he woke in the night; I can relate to that in the days before our kids started to sleep through. And when you do get up and go the bathroom there's nothing quite like your 18 month old son coming up behind you and trying to push his way between your legs as you're trying to take a pee; if you're not already fully awake that will do it for you!

For all the things we've been through and done together, I know how incredibly lucky I've been to have found such a great woman with whom to share life and make a family; hopefully all the better for some basic fatherly wisdom that to make it work for both of us takes not only love but effort, patience and understanding. There are still frequent occasions when my wife will say she's better equipped than me, but in this modern world mere men can only do their best!

EYE EYE

Charles Bristow

(as narrated to another breakfast boy)

There is frequently a fine dividing line between desire and necessity and this perhaps may best be illustrated by something unfortunate that happened to someone else. An acquaintance of mine once suffered what seems to have become an increasingly common problem, to whit, a detached retina. The unlikely chances of this occurring increase with the onset of two factors. The first is the ever popular habit and sport of hurling oneself off an unbelievably high structure tethered only, for the sake of safety, with a string of elastic round the ankles; the second is age, since with this the fault arises from the continued increase in viscosity of the vitreous humour (the jelly like filling side the eye). When this happens the rear coating of the eye (the retina) sometimes catches to it, sticks and tears.

Well, it did. At the time and for some days following nothing seemed to be wrong, but then, very slowly a thin veil seemed to creep across the eye, restricting vision and causing great alarm to the poor sufferer. The net result of this spread panic into the household and a trip to the doctors resulted in a rapid escalation to the local hospital where the diagnosis was relatively easy, the solution well known and a date for the operation readily arranged. All seemed fine until the actual day arrived and the patient, being somewhat agitated over the prospects of someone messing around with an eye, sat white faced and trembling in pre-op.

The surgeon had already explained about the problem, the solution, and the method in some detail so there was no element of doubt on that score. However, as the moment of truth arrived the great man wanted to know that the patient, obviously in some distress, understood all that was about to happen. He once more ran through the proposals, explaining not only the procedure in all its gory detail but ran round the members of the theatre team and explained their various roles, right down to the pretty little nurse whose job it was just to hold his hand in a gesture of comfort.

At length, with the deadline reached, a nursing sister arrived with what looked like a garden syringe and explained that her job was to inject the first of the anaesthetics through the front of the eye. The patient held up his hand in a demonstration of unreadiness, hesitated for just a moment or two before asking the salient but unlikely question 'Is there any chance you could go in from the back?'

DON'T SHOOT THE MESSENGER

Ian Frearson

There was a time when all Anglican churches appeared to enjoy the privilege of an extensive staff. Although not completely familiar with the system, being a Primitive Methodist, I was aware that our local vicar also had a curate. The one I remember made quite a mark when he arrived. First of all, he was dressed very casually in a sports jacket that did not sport leather patches, up-to-the-minute slacks and an open necked shirt. Secondly he was young – very young – and to the greatest consternation of many of us lads he was very good looking. His 6ft frame displayed his broad shoulders, narrow hips and a tousled heard of straw blond hair that was always unruly – but delightfully so. I hated him.

During the next few weeks I hated him even more since he exhibited a friendly outlook to all including the females, the young ones in particular. He spent some time each day in his keep fit regime and running.

Alfreton Park was at that time still in the ownership of the Squire who, it appeared, had given his permission for the Curate to go wherever he liked on the estate. We all thought it was his wife's doing. This resulted in my not only running but pursuing other activities that demonstrated his prowess. Gosh we hated him. Basically he was a young Adonis, but seemed oblivious to the signs, smiles and alluring glances that came his way. All it seemed he had time for was his work in the church and to this he set forth with a will and vigour that required all his stamina and fitness. It was his downfall in the end.

One Sunday, a fateful day in his calendar, he strode up to the pulpit like a young god, hair flying out behind, long legs powerfully carrying him forward to his goal like the young buck he was, ascended the steps to make his announcements. It was then that he fell. The start was pretty good. His comments on the various events he planned or with which he was already involved, were accepted by the womenfolk with sighs, titters and coy glances as he gave out both information, thanks and compliments alike, then he paused.

'There is one area in which I feel I have failed', he stated. Everyone suddenly froze. Was this his Achilles heel? Had he not lived up to their expectations? The best was yet to come as he carried on falling on his sword by uttering these fatal words. 'I am so very disappointed, saddened and surprised, despite my long perseverance and tireless efforts, to see so few young mothers here'. He left the following week with the sound of laughter still ringing in his ears.

MY FATHER JUDAH

Peter Dawson

Judah Dawson was one of thirteen children fathered by Isaac Davidson, an impoverished Jew of the diaspora, the dispersion. Isaac came to England some time in the nineteenth century. He attenuated his name to Dawson for reasons unknown and married Mary O'Connell, a girl who had fled a life of grinding poverty in Ireland. How the two met is not known but they raised their family in the East End of London.

Born in 1900, Judah grew up a street urchin within the sound of Bow Bells. In adulthood, his speech was a mixture of cockney slang and yiddisher from his Jewish heritage. On the one hand, he called his socks his almond rocks and on the other he described anyone he didn't like as a schmuk.

Chasing round the streets of the East End as a boy, he and his mates used to run into the main road and jump on the backs of lorries for a free ride. One day Judah fell off under the wheels of a tram and lost most of one foot, so he never did any military service.

Not long after the outbreak of war in 1939 with a German invasion seemingly imminent my father abandoned the name Judah and called himself Richard. When asked why, he said, 'We're not going to no concentrated camp'.

My father's Jewish roots were most clearly exposed when the extended family was gathered on special occasions. Then it was that Dickie Dawson's skill as a teller of Jewish jokes was celebrated.

Someone would demand that he told the tale of Yossel and Schmulick. I can hear his voice now as he regaled the company.

Yossel and Schmulick are sitting in the synagogue on the Sabbath. While the rabbi reads from the holy scroll, Schmulick shuffles his feet and groans. Afterwards, Yossel asks, 'For why were you shuffling your feet?' Schmulick explains that his shoes are too tight and are crippling him. 'Then why don't you get some shoes that fit?' exclaims Yossel. 'Well,' replies Schmulick, 'it's like this. My son has dropped out of university; my daughter, would you believe, wants to marry a goy, a gentile; the roof of my house leaks; my business is failing and my wife never stops nagging me. My whole life is a disaster. But when I get home from my day's work and take my shoes off, for a few moments, I feel wonderful'.

In adulthood, he who had been Judah and was now known as Dickie Dawson worked nights at the *Daily Express* in Fleet Street, tying up packs of newspapers as they rolled off the presses and loading them into vans for distribution to newsagents across the country. If any part of the process of writing, typesetting, printing, packing and distribution the paper, so that copies were on newsagents' doorsteps by first light failed, the editor would go berserk.

This gave the print unions enormous power. Dickie Dawson was father of the chapel in the *Daily Express* warehouse. It was not a religious appointment. He was shop steward. Back in the 1950s, Fleet Street shop stewards were more powerful than the newspaper owners, who lived in fear of losing a day's sales.

Dickie looked just like the American film star James Cagney. If a Cagney film was on at our local cinema, he insisted on taking us to see it. When we were coming out at the end, people would look at my dad and do a double take. He loved that.

He was envious of my spending two years in the military when I was called up for National Service at eighteen. My dad, with his crippled foot, thought square bashing and being shouted at by drill corporals sounded great fun. On leave at the end of recruit training, I related how I had once failed to swing my arms sufficiently when marching. An NCO bringing has face close up to mine, bawled, 'If you don't get those arms moving, airman, I'll pull one of 'em off and beat your bloody head in with the soggy end'. Being just out of the sixth form and rather full of myself after getting good A Level results, I felt like saying, 'Well my good man, my head certainly would be bloody if you did that', but I wisely declined. Father wished he could have had such an experience. For him, the grass was greener on the side of the street where men with two feet marched.

My father died at 62 of lung cancer. Like many working class men of his time, he was a chain smoker. I was at his bedside when he died at home, the hospital surgeons having opened him up, shaken their heads in despair, sewn him up again and sent him home to die. His lungs were a labyrinth of nicotine. He was spewing up a thick stream of the stuff as he breathed his last.

Dickie Dawson was a compulsive gambler. You could say that he had the last laugh with the bookies. Three weeks before he died, he placed £10 on a horse called Kilmore for the Grand National, which was five weeks away. Because he placed the bet so long in advance, he got odds of ten to one. By the time of the race, Kilmore was second favourite at six to four. When it won, my widowed mother received a hundred pounds from dad's bookmaker. She said, 'That's nice. It's the most money I've ever had off him from his gambling. God bless the old sod'. And so said all of us who knew and loved him.

THIS IS NOT THE WAY IT SHOULD BE

Anon

It's not the way it should be
You look so fit and well, sound so relaxed
and yet –
there is that distance between us like I have
never known.
It's not as if you wanted it like this
Not as if you organised it to be so, and yet
there still is that distance between us
like I have never known.

You speak of the mundane – of shopping
for essentials,
getting by on less by far than I can imagine
being possible.
Is this the thing that keeps the distance
between us
like I have never known

This Is Not the Way It Should Be

I sit in awe, relaxed, cocooned,
softly surrounding settee makes me prickle
with discomfort
as you tell, despite all, the ways that things
get done,
like I have never known.

It's not the way it should be
Flies and beetles sharing food that only earlier
this day
was so carefully chosen, slaughtered and
held aloft
for you to inspect, decide, invest.

So tell it on for it's not the way it should be.
After all the work you invested to see
that others
had a chance to rise from the poverty
and squalor
like I have never known

It's not the way it should be
The growls and squeals of blackest night, the
bleats of panic
die away to wait for dawn to reveal the sight,
A trail of blood, a spoor to indicate the villain,
chased, secured, devoured, the kill
is vindicated.

This Is Not the Way It Should Be

It's not the way it should be
I need to see your face to feel your mind
To know your spirits peace, to touch your hand
and yet
you are your father's son and so it has to be
despite my thoughts
That this is not the way it should be.

Come home soon